HOW THE
WHITE HOUSE
REALLY WORKS

HOW THE WHITE HOUSE REALLY WORKS

George Sullivan

SCHOLASTIC INC.
New York Toronto London Auckland Sydney

Cover photo credit: Henryk Kaiser / Leo de Wys Inc.

Frontispiece photo credit: George Sullivan

ISBN 0-590-43403-9

12 11 10 9 8 7 6 5   2 3 4 5/9

Printed in the U.S.A.   08

First Scholastic printing, January 1990

Acknowledgments

A great many people contributed information and photographs for use in this book. Special thanks are due Gary J. Walters, Chief Usher, the White House; Anne Higgins, Special Assistant to the President and Director of Correspondence; Larry M. Speakes, former Deputy Press Secretary; Carol McKay, White House Photo Laboratory; Martin I. Elzy, Jimmy Carter Library; Richard L. Holzhausen, Gerald R. Ford Library; Allan B. Goodrich, John Fitzgerald Kennedy Library; Benedict H. Zobrist, Harry S. Truman Library; Martin M. Teasley, Dwight D. Eisenhower Library; Mark Renovitch, Franklin D. Roosevelt Library; E. Philip Scott, Lyndon Baines Johnson Library; and James E. Detlefsen, Herbert Hoover Library.

Special thanks are also due Ellen V. LiBretto; Linda Mohler, *Parade* Magazine; Francesca Kurti, TLC Custom Labs; Herman Darvick, Universal Autograph Collectors Club; Trish Gallagher, Bruce Pluckhahn, Paula McMartin, and Tim Sullivan.

Contents

Introduction

When Ronald Reagan became president in 1981, his move into the White House triggered boyhood memories of the time his father ran a business out of the family home in Tampico, Illinois. Like that home, the White House was going to be Mr. Reagan's combined work place and residence. "I'm back living above the store again," Mr. Reagan joked.

It's true. The White House, the world-famous mansion in Washington, D.C., is where the president of the United States both lives and works. Often called the Executive Mansion, it contains not only the living quarters for the president and his family but the offices where he and his staff and the first lady and her staff conduct official business.

Sometimes it also serves as a guest hotel, with rooms set aside for visitors of state or the first family's relatives and friends.

And, of course, the White House is a national monument with certain rooms on the ground floor and first floor open to visitors. Priceless works of art are displayed in these rooms.

About one million tourists parade through the mansion each year.

In recent times, the White House has become like a fortress, staffed with armed guards and fitted out with the latest security devices for protecting the lives of the first family.

The job of president of the United States has been called the toughest in the world. But living in the White House provides certain comforts and conveniences. The president and first lady are surrounded by clusters of butlers, housemaids, cooks, plumbers, and carpenters—close to a hundred household employees.

There are limousines, helicopters, and jets for travel. There is a barbershop for trims and, for the president's wife, a beauty salon. There is a professionally staffed medical clinic to help keep the president and his family healthy.

Concerts and parties provide entertainment. Fine meals are prepared for visiting dignitaries, and a cellar is stocked with the best American wines. There are a gym for exercise, a tennis court, a bowling alley, and a movie theater.

This book tells how the White House operates as a home and office, as a museum and tourist attraction. In so doing, it gives a behind-the-scenes look at life within the official residence of the president of the United States.

— 1 —
People in Power

Everyone knows about the Oval Office, the office in the West Wing of the White House where the president works, reading reports and proposed legislation, signing documents, and meeting with staff members. Less well known is the Rectangular Office—several rooms, actually—in the southwest corner of the West Wing. This is where the president's chief of staff presides.

From the Oval Office, the president looks out upon spacious lawns studded with trees and tall shrubbery and, beyond, the Washington Monument. The chief of staff's view is more down-to-earth. He looks out upon West Executive Avenue, which is closed to the public. The blacktop has been marked off with numbered parking spaces, often occupied with the limousines of officials making White House visits.

Donald T. Regan, who was President Reagan's chief of staff from 1985 until he resigned his post in February 1987, had power second only to the president himself. A take-charge man, he liked to describe himself as the one person

1

President Ronald Reagan *(right)* meets with Chief of Staff Donald Regan *(second from right)* and other top advisers *(left to right)* Caspar Weinberger, secretary of defense; George Shultz, secretary of state; and Edwin Meese, attorney general.   THE WHITE HOUSE / PETE SOUZA

who knew the full story of what was going on at the White House.

From the time his chauffeur-driven blue limousine pulled into the west basement of the White House each morning at 7:15 A.M., until his day ended almost twelve hours later, he was in personal control of the operation of the entire White House.

He met with the president at least six times a day. He controlled the president's daily schedule and decided what trips the president was to make. He decided whom the president was to see. He cleared the president's phone calls and decided what letters and memos the president should read.

He supervised the writing of the president's speeches. He advised the president when he was required to appoint someone to an important position.

He helped the president reach all major decisions, providing him with the background information he needed in each case.

He sat in on all cabinet meetings and National Security Council sessions. He attended legislative strategy meetings, budget review conferences, and meetings with congressional leaders. He was said to exercise some degree of influence over every aspect of domestic and foreign policy.

He was honest and straightforward, brash and blunt.

When things went wrong, he often stepped forward to take the heat, which did nothing to boost his popularity. "If someone gets a cold in this town," he once said, "I get the blame."

Across West Executive Avenue is the Old Executive Office Building—called the Old E.O.B.—a hulking gray granite mass that was known as the State, Navy, and War Building up until the 1940s. All of the president's top aides, or assistants, work in the West Wing of the White House. But hundreds of others have their offices in the Old Executive Office Building. (There's also a New Executive Office Building, but it is not part of the White House complex.)

The president's aides help in performing every aspect of the president's job. They assist him in formulating foreign policy and domestic programs. They help develop legislation and then work to steer the legislation through Congress. They provide information and suggestions to help the president make decisions. They write the president's speeches. They handle his day-to-day dealings with the news media.

Hamilton Jordan *(left)* served as a top aide to President Jimmy Carter.   JIMMY CARTER LIBRARY

Presidential aides work long hours, beginning early in the morning and often continuing until late at night. They often work six and sometimes seven days a week. The homes of senior members of the staff are equipped with direct telephone lines to the White House so the president can reach them at any time of the day or night.

A lot of perquisites, however, go with the job. A perquisite —perk, for short—is a fringe benefit, something over and above one's salary.

Senior officials get big offices. The General Services Administration (GSA)—which manages all government property and records, including buildings—has established regulations concerning office size. A high-ranking presidential aide is entitled to an office that is 750 square feet in size, which is about twice as big as the average living room. His or her domain also includes a 50-square-foot kitchen, a 300-square-foot dining area, and a 45-square-foot bathroom.

An executive aide has a car or driver at his or her disposal. A top official gets a limousine. But even a lowly member of the White House staff gets an official car that is chauffeured by an army sergeant.

A high-ranking member of the White House staff can dine at the wood-paneled White House Mess. Just a floor below the Oval Office, it is comparable to a fine restaurant. If a telephone call comes for an aide during the meal, a member of the mess staff brings a phone to the table.

There is also a special dining room for those who don't quite rate the White House Mess. Officials of lower status take their meals in the executive dining room of the Old Executive Office Building.

Another perk is the business card that is issued to presidential staffers. It is inscribed with the person's name and the magic words THE WHITE HOUSE. A person who flashes such a card never has to wait in line at a movie theater or anywhere else, and is practically guaranteed the best table in any restaurant.

The idea of a president having a staff of hundreds and a chief, such as Donald Regan, to run it is relatively new. Up until the time of Franklin D. Roosevelt, the president had no staff as we know it today. The president usually got things done through the men and women who headed the Executive Department of the government. Together, the heads of the Executive Department are known as the president's cabinet.

These are the thirteen Executive Departments:

AGRICULTURE
COMMERCE
DEFENSE
EDUCATION
ENERGY
HEALTH AND HUMAN SERVICES
HOUSING AND URBAN DEVELOPMENT
THE INTERIOR
JUSTICE
LABOR
STATE
TRANSPORTATION
THE TREASURY

Some departments are huge. The Department of Defense, for example, has approximately a million employees.

Important changes in how the president runs things were made under Franklin Roosevelt, who served three full terms and part of a fourth.

Roosevelt became president in 1933, during the Great Depression. To combat unemployment and the business slump, Roosevelt launched a wide range of government programs. One result was that the federal government started playing a major role in the nation's economy.

Many of the advisers who helped Roosevelt in his presidential campaign stayed on to assist him after he entered the White House. These aides included Harry Hopkins, Samuel Rosenman, and Rexford Rugwell. The group was known as Roosevelt's brain trust.

Roosevelt was still president in 1939 when World War II began. The United States entered the war in 1941. World

President Franklin D. Roosevelt *(left)* with Harry Hopkins,
a member of his brain trust

War II further expanded the role of the presidency in both domestic and international affairs.

In 1939, Roosevelt created the Executive Office of the President. Today, this division has more than two thousand employees. The agencies that make up the Executive Office of the President include the Office of Management and Budget, the National Security Council, the Council of Economic Advisers, and the Office of Science and Technology Policy.

When Harry S. Truman succeeded Roosevelt as president in 1945, the Executive Office staff numbered only 225 employees. Truman added to it, although very slowly.

During Truman's administration, many members of the president's staff were shifted from the White House across West Executive Avenue to what is now known as the Old

Most presidential aides have their offices in the Old Executive Office Building, which is just west of the White House.

Executive Office Building. The avenue was closed to traffic to permit easy movement between the two buildings.

The trend toward using a personal staff to get things accomplished received a big boost under Dwight D. Eisenhower, who became president in 1953.

All of his adult life, Eisenhower had been a military leader. As such, he had always relied upon a staff, a group of officers who assisted him in planning and other matters.

"Where's my staff?" Eisenhower asked when he took over the presidency. "There is no staff," he was told. Whereupon, Eisenhower made each cabinet officer as well as other executives responsible for an area of government affairs. He named Sherman Adams, who had served as a representative in Con-

President Dwight D. Eisenhower *(center)* with Chief of Staff
Sherman Adams *(right)* and other aides

President John F. Kennedy *(right)* with Chief of Staff Theodore Sorensen in 1963

gress and as governor of New Hampshire, to be his chief of staff.

In the years since Eisenhower, the size and importance of the White House staff has grown by leaps and bounds. For example, during the 1970s, when Richard M. Nixon was president, national economic policy was determined by four people. Only one, the secretary of the treasury, was a member of Nixon's cabinet. The noncabinet appointees whom Nixon relied upon were the chief of the Council of Economic Advisers, the director of the Office of Management and Budget, and the head of the Federal Reserve Board.

Many people criticize the practice of using staff members to help run domestic and international affairs. Doing so, they say, undermines the power of the members of the cabinet.

That's not the only problem. When the president wants to fill a cabinet post, he nominates someone. That individual must then be approved by the Senate.

But the president simply appoints his chief of staff and other aides. They do not have to be examined by the Senate. Some people say that this violates the spirit of the Constitution, which dictates that the president make appointments with the advice and consent of the Senate.

Another problem with the present system, critics say, is that White House staff members often lack training and experience. Every president wants to make a fresh start. He has new ideas; he is eager to launch new programs. So the new president brings in new people, from his chief of staff right down to the clerical workers. Because these people have no background in running the government, they are not always effective in their jobs. Sometimes they make mistakes.

On the other hand, the Department of State, the Department of Agriculture, and other executive departments of the government are staffed by career professionals. It doesn't matter who happens to be president; they stay in their jobs from one administration to the next. They are fully trained and experienced.

Twice in recent years, the staff system is said to have contributed to crises in government. During the administration of Richard Nixon, the presidency was damaged by the Watergate scandal. Top presidential aides were convicted of bri-

H. R. Haldeman, a top aide to President Nixon, listens to a
question before the Senate Watergate Committee in 1973.

bery, fraud, and the obstruction of justice, and sent to prison.
On August 9, 1974, Mr. Nixon, facing possible impeachment,
resigned as president.

During Ronald Reagan's second term in office, presidential
aides operating out of an office in the White House basement
were found to have entered into secret arms negotiations with
Iran. Millions of dollars from the Iranians were sent to the

"freedom fighters" in Nicaragua. President Reagan said he "was not fully informed" as to what had happened. The incident scarred the presidency.

Despite these crises, no one foresees great change. The next president, like every president since Dwight Eisenhower, is sure to appoint a chief of staff and give him enormous power. Dozens of other advisers and assistants will also be appointed. More and more, it is by means of the staff system that the White House conducts official business.

2

Keeping in Touch

Every day, many thousands of Americans reach out to their leader. They seek to share with him their ideas and opinions, their dreams and frustrations. They write to him; they telephone him.

The letters and telephone calls that pour into the White House in a year's time number well into the millions. Despite this flood, no letter goes unacknowledged, no telephone call goes unanswered.

During the administration of Ronald Reagan, some 12,000 to 20,000 pieces of mail reached the White House daily. The amount was often influenced by major news events. President Reagan's policies in the Persian Gulf or his Supreme Court appointments caused a sharp increase in the amount of mail he received. News stories about his and Mrs. Reagan's health also triggered more letters.

In writing to the president, some people criticize; others offer their support. Often the letters are very personal, talking about the writers' families, their jobs, and their hopes for the future.

A sampling of the 12,000 to 20,000 letters received daily by
the Reagan White House

All letters addressed to the president or first lady get deliv-
ered to the White House Office of Correspondence on the
fourth floor of the Old Executive Office Building. During
Ronald Reagan's term, the office was staffed by approximately 130 employees, plus some 450 volunteers.

All incoming mail is read and the subject of each letter is
noted. Computers are used to record this information, and also
to answer the correspondence. "Everything's electronic," said
Anne Higgins, director of the White House Office of Correspondence, who also supervised correspondence for Richard
Nixon and Gerald Ford. "Installing computers was one of the
big changes made during Mr. Reagan's administration."

Naturally, neither the president nor the first lady can per-

Anne Higgins served as Director of Correspondence during the Ford, Nixon, and Reagan administrations.

sonally answer all the letters each receives. A previously prepared letter or printed card is often sent in reply. For instance, when someone writes the president to congratulate him on his birthday or a wedding anniversary, that person gets a printed message expressing the president's thanks.

Some of the letters to the president contain a problem or a question. These letters are routed to the government agency best able to handle them. For instance, suppose a person writes to complain that he or she is being treated unfairly at work. Such a letter is likely to be sent to the appropriate division of the Department of Labor.

Letters that praise or criticize the president for the way he is handling a particular matter are answered by letter. But most such letters of response are likely to be identical. Only the addresses are different.

Someone requesting an autograph of the president may receive in response a small card about the size of a standard business card. It bears the words THE WHITE HOUSE and a printed signature of the president.

Packages sent to the president are X-rayed for reasons of security. Any suspicious package is immediately handed over to the Secret Service. Any threatening letters go to the Secret Service, too.

Most of the packages contain gifts. Many of the gifts are handmade items. The president sends a printed thank-you message for each gift he receives. The gifts are stored. Later, when the president leaves office and a library is established for his letters and documents, the gifts become a part of the library collection.

Mail from children is handled by a special staff of five. President Reagan received as many as four thousand letters a week from boys and girls. All letters were answered, unless the

Your kind message of birthday greetings means a great deal to me. Thank you very much for your thoughtfulness.

Dwight D Eisenhower

Thank you for remembering us at Christmas time. We send our best wishes for a New Year of happiness and fulfillment.

Lady Bird Johnson

Lyndon B Johnson

Nancy and I are deeply touched by the way so many people have reached out to us during these days. My recovery has been hastened and my spirits uplifted by the many good wishes that have come my way from friends like you. From the bottom of my heart, thank you and God bless you.

Ronald Reagan

THE WHITE HOUSE
WASHINGTON

Best wishes from Richard Nixon

Sometimes cards like this one are sent to those
who request autographs.

writer failed to include a return address or the handwriting
was so poor that the message couldn't be read.

Many boys and girls ask personal questions of the president. Favorite questions include:

> What are your hobbies?
> How many pets live at the White House?
> How much salary do you receive?
> Were you ever a Boy Scout?
> What are some of your favorite foods?
> Are there really ghosts in the White House?

During the administration of Ronald Reagan, youngsters
asking such questions received in reply a handsome twenty-
eight-page booklet with color photographs, titled *The President's House.* It contained historical information about the
White House and biographical notes about the president and
the first lady, plus answers to the most frequently asked questions.

◀— Many letters are answered with printed messages like these.

Youngsters writing to ask questions concerning current events usually received an eight-page illustrated newsletter in reply. It explained the president's position on whatever topic had been raised. Among the subjects discussed were Central America, financial aid for college students, and prayer in the schools.

Occasionally, children send gifts to the president. In 1981, when President Reagan was in the hospital recovering from an assassination attempt, ten-year-old Barnaby Bullard of Loudonville, New York, sent a goldfish, packing it in a plastic bag filled with water. The fish managed to arrive safely at the White House Office of Correspondence. There it occupied a tank bearing the presidential seal. The staff referred to it as the "first fish."

Whether the reply from the president goes to a child or an adult, only a tiny percentage of all letters are actually signed by the chief executive himself. Instead, letters are mechanically signed by a device called the Autopen.

John F. Kennedy was the first president to use an Autopen. It consists of an electrically powered metal arm with a pen mounted at one end. Beneath the arm there's a die, or matrix, cut to match a sample of the person's signature.

The operator places the letter beneath the pen and presses a foot pedal, which causes the matrix to revolve and guide the pen across the paper. The Autopen can produce hundreds of signatures in an hour.

Many different versions of the president's signature can be used. President Reagan had about a dozen Autopen patterns. There were several versions of *Ronald Reagan,* plus a *Ronnie* and a *Ron.* For close friends, there was said to be a *Dutch,* Mr. Reagan's nickname.

One of Ronald Reagan's Autopen signatures

Not only presidents use the Autopen, incidentally. Hundreds of such machines are signing away in Washington. They are used by representatives, senators, cabinet officers, Supreme Court justices, and other officials.

President Jimmy Carter relied upon proxy signatures as well as on the Autopen. Secretaries in Mr. Carter's office sometimes signed his name to official correspondence. Herman Darvick, president of the Universal Autograph Collectors Club, once noted that Susan Clough, Mr. Carter's personal secretary, "forged his name beautifully."

During the mid-1980s, Autopens began to be replaced by computer-generated signatures. In the years ahead, the Autopen may go the way of the rubber-stamp signature, once used by President Andrew Johnson after he had suffered an arm injury.

Not all letters to the president get a form reply or an Autopen signature. During the time Ronald Reagan was president, Anne Higgins used to pick out a batch of letters every couple of weeks and send them to the Oval Office. They were chosen as representative of the topics people were writing about at the time. President Reagan personally replied to about thirty of these letters. He wrote his responses in longhand on yellow legal-sized paper. A secretary typed them. The original handwritten versions were sent to the National Archives.

"The president takes a tremendous interest in his correspondence," said Ms. Higgins. "He seems to love answering letters, which is hard to believe when you're getting so much mail."

Tucked away in a pleasant office with white walls and beige carpeting in a subbasement of the Old Executive Office Building is the White House switchboard, staffed by twenty telephone operators. They work in eight-hour shifts, around the clock.

The White House telephone number—(202) 456-1414—is no secret. It is no wonder that the switchboard has to deal with about fifty thousand calls a day. About thirty thousand are for the president.

During emergencies, the number of calls shoots up. On the August day in 1974 when Richard Nixon resigned as president, more than 102,000 calls were received. The lines were also jammed after the space shuttle *Challenger* exploded on takeoff in 1985.

Of course, calls to the president have to be sorted out. The operator who gets the call doesn't know who is on the other end. It could be a White House official or a concerned citizen, a close personal friend of the president or someone playing a joke.

In screening the president's callers, the operator often asks the caller's whereabouts and gets a home or office number that can be verified. Suppose Senator Edward Kennedy is calling the president. The operator takes down the senator's number and checks it against the files. Once it is established as legitimate, the operator calls the senator back. Says one operator: "It would be almost impossible for a caller to misrepresent

President Gerald Ford chats with an operator at the White House switchboard during a tour of the Old Executive Office Building in 1974. GERALD R. FORD LIBRARY

himself or herself and get all the way through to the president."

Most of the odd calls the switchboard receives are from jokers. But occasionally a caller voices a threat against the president. Such calls are routed instantly to the Secret Service.

Most of the fifty thousand or so people who call the White House on the average day are simply American citizens who have something they want to tell the president or first lady. These callers are switched to the Comment and Greeting Office, which is staffed by volunteers, mostly retired government workers. Each caller is treated courteously. As for collect calls, the White House never accepts them.

When it comes to outgoing calls, the operators pride themselves on fast service. They maintain a file of thousands of telephone numbers. It includes the names of heads of state, current and former government officials, business leaders, journalists and, of course, friends and associates of the president and first lady.

The operators keep the file up-to-date by reading newspapers and magazines. If someone is being considered for an important government job, his or her telephone number goes into the file.

"We'll check the newspapers to find out if a big football game is scheduled," one operator says. "We'll make a note of the names of the coaches and where the game is being played. The president, you see, might want to speak with one or both of them after the game. He often does, and we're ready with the number."

The White House operators have earned legendary fame for tracking down just about anyone the president or first lady wants to talk to. When Nancy Reagan wanted to speak with Sheila Tate, her vacationing press secretary, Ms. Tate was picked up at her beach house in New Jersey by a police patrol car and driven to the station house so she could place a call to the White House.

John F. Kennedy once tested the operators' skills and determination by asking them to track down a member of his staff—who was standing at JFK's elbow. It was no contest. The operators had their man within minutes.

The operators have gotten in touch with men on trains and told them to get off at the next station to accept a White House call. They have called airport managers and had them hold planes until a staffer could get to the phone.

Dwight D. Eisenhower once wanted to speak to a foreign-policy consultant. The man was on a deep-sea fishing expedi-

In 1955, during the administration of Dwight D. Eisenhower, the White House switchboard looked like this.

tion and couldn't be reached. The operators became desperate. One of them finally got someone to attach a note to a tree near the spot where the aide's boat was going to dock. When he came ashore, there was the note, and he immediately placed the call.

Should the president wish to speak with the leader of the Soviet Union, he can do so by means of the hot line, a two-way telegraph-teleprinter system that links the White House and the Kremlin. Established in 1963, the hot line enables the two leaders to communicate directly and instantly in the case of an international crisis. Its intention, of course, is to reduce the risk of war triggered by a misunderstanding.

Lyndon Johnson was said to have used the telephone more than any other president. LYNDON BAINES JOHNSON LIBRARY

White House operators agree that Lyndon Johnson used the telephone more than any other president. He often was on the telephone from 8:00 A.M. to midnight. He once told his daughter Luci that if the White House operators couldn't find someone, they weren't findable.

John F. Kennedy was addicted to the telephone, too. He said that there were two things he would like to take from the White House when he returned to private life. One was the president's plane, *Air Force One*; the other was the White House switchboard.

The switchboard operators often become deeply attached to the members of the first family. On November 4, 1980, President Jimmy Carter ran for reelection against Ronald Reagan. When it appeared that Mr. Reagan had built an insurmountable lead, Mr. Carter asked Operator One (the title of the operator assigned to the president) to put in a call to Mr. Reagan so he could concede the election. "I couldn't believe it. I was afraid I was going to cry," the operator recalled. "Making that call was the hardest thing I ever did in my life."

The first telephone was installed in the White House in 1878, during Rutherford B. Hayes's term of office. The device was not quickly accepted. Theodore Roosevelt disliked the telephone so much he used it only in emergencies. Woodrow Wilson hated the telephone, and he issued orders that the operators were *not* to ring him.

—3—
Upstairs at the White House

Early each morning, Tuesday through Saturday, the tourists line up two and three abreast on the sidewalk that stretches south of the White House's East Gate, awaiting ten o'clock and the beginning of the public tours. (Tourists may also take special White House tours by obtaining passes from their senators or representatives.) Some twenty thousand sightseers stream through the White House each week during peak periods of the tourist season.

Guards check each person's bags and belongings. Everyone must be electronically screened for weapons. No photo-taking is permitted during the tour.

Once they have completed the security check, the tourists enter the East Wing on the ground floor in groups of thirty to forty. Then they go into the mansion. They see the library, with its more than 2,700 books describing various aspects of American life. They see the Vermeil Room, where gilded silver—vermeil—is exhibited on the shelves. Most of the pieces are used for state luncheons and dinners.

Sightseers enter the White House through the East Gate.

29

Then the tourists walk up a flight of marble stairs to the first floor, which is called the State Floor. They file through the Green Room, Blue Room, Red Room, and the State Dining Room, a large room with space enough for 140 guests at large dinners or luncheons.

In the various rooms, the tourists see antique furniture, paintings, and elegant wall coverings. Many are struck by a sense of history. They speak in hushed tones.

After leaving the State Dining Room, each group follows its guide through a wide hallway to the other end of the mansion and the East Room, the largest room in the White House. The East Room is used for receptions, the staging of entertainment, and for press conferences. It has also been the scene of several White House weddings, including that of Lynda Bird Johnson.

After visiting the East Room, the tourists spill out onto the North Portico. Most pause there to pose for snapshots with the stately white columns as a backdrop.

Then they amble down the curving walkway that leads to the northeast pedestrian gate and Pennsylvania Avenue. When they return home, they tell their relatives and friends that they have visited the president's house.

And indeed they have. But they have seen only a small portion of it.

What the tour groups never see are the upstairs rooms of the White House—those used by the president, the president's family, their guests, and the president's staff. These rooms, found on the second and third floors, are off limits to all but a very few.

The second floor contains the living quarters of the president and the first family. Such notable rooms as the Treaty Room, the Queen's Bedroom, and the Lincoln Bedroom are on the east end of the second floor.

Mrs. Gerald Ford on a tour of the White House living quarters conducted by Chief Usher Rex Scouten on August 13, 1974 GERALD R. FORD LIBRARY

Richard Nixon used the Lincoln Sitting Room as his private room. He kept a fire burning in the grate year round, even in the summer when the air-conditioning was on. He sometimes smoked cigars there and occasionally set off the White House fire alarm doing so.

The ghost of Lincoln has been said to inhabit the room. Amy Carter and her friends once tried to get in touch with Lincoln with a Ouija board, but were not successful. The Reagans' dog sometimes barked at the door of the room but shied away from entering it.

At the west end of the second floor, the president and his wife have several rooms as their own. President and Mrs. Nixon originally used one of the rooms as a bedroom, one as a study, and a third as a dressing room. But before long, Mrs.

Nixon moved out of their bedroom into the second room. She said that the president liked to wake up in the middle of the night to read or work, and she couldn't sleep with the light on.

Like the Fords and the Carters, the Reagans shared a bedroom and used the other room as a sitting room. The dressing room is traditionally the first lady's. Each room has a bath.

At the northwest corner of the second floor are the president's dining room and a small kitchen, which used to be a bedroom suite. The suite was converted to its present use by Mrs. Kennedy, who found it inconvenient to feed her young children, John and Caroline, on the first floor in what is called the Family Dining Room.

The third floor has two suites of rooms, two guest rooms, a laundry, an ironing room, and a changing room for the servants. It was on the third floor that President Reagan spent much of his time while recovering from the wound he received during the assassination attempt in 1981.

Up a ramp to the flat roof is the Solarium, perhaps the cheeriest room in the White House. Its glass walls keep the room flooded with sunlight. The room originated during the administration of Calvin Coolidge. Mrs. Coolidge called the Solarium the sky parlor. The Kennedy children had their schooling there. Rosalynn Carter called it her favorite room for living. On the other side of the roof is a greenhouse.

Not only are tourists not permitted to see the private rooms of the White House, they also never get a chance to see the White House at work. While a sightseer may catch a glimpse of a presidential aide or the White House doorman, seldom do visitors ever see the men and women who are charged with keeping the president's residence running smoothly.

The domestic and maintenance staff, most of whom carry

The Solarium was Rosalynn Carter's favorite room for living.

WIDE WORLD

over from one administration to the next, is made up of nine-ty-three employees. This includes three ushers, an administrative assistant, an accountant, eight housemaids, seven house-men, one maitre d', six butlers, three chefs, three cooks, three doormen, two laundresses, two pantrymen, an executive housekeeper, and engineers and painters.

The person who is responsible for the operation of the White House—supervising and directing all the employees—is the chief usher. A kind of White House general manager, the chief usher rarely gets mentioned in the newspapers and is never seen on television; yet the White House could not operate efficiently without him.

He is the financial officer of the Executive Mansion, preparing the budget and controlling expenditures for food and supplies.

He is in charge of receiving and caring for all personal and official guests who call on the president and first lady. He

33

makes arrangements for receptions, dinners, and official entertainment. He is in charge of the day-to-day maintenance of the mansion, its cleaning and upkeep.

J. B. West, who retired in 1969 after twenty-eight years at the White House, first as an assistant usher and later as chief usher, was asked many times, "What does a chief usher do?"

Mr. West usually replied, "I do what I'm told to do."

The position of chief usher is unique. As Gary J. Walters, who became chief usher in 1986, has pointed out, "There's not another house in the world that serves as a home for a president or head of state and that is open to the public on a regular basis—and is also a museum. There are no schools or university courses to teach a person how to run such a place. There's no way to get the necessary experience—except through on-the-job training, that is, by working at the White House itself."

Mr. Walters was an assistant usher at the White House for ten years before becoming chief usher. Before that, he served as a member of the White House Secret Service team assigned to guard the president.

The term *chief usher* dates to a much earlier day, to the time when the president's office was contained in the residence—that is, before the White House's West Wing was built. Guests would arrive at the North Portico and be escorted upstairs to the president's office by an usher.

After Theodore Roosevelt moved into the White House in 1901, he ordered new offices for the president in the West Wing. Work on them was completed in 1902. Although the chief usher has taken on countless other duties and responsibilities since that time, the title has remained the same.

Besides supervising the regular staff, the chief usher is also

Gary J. Walters became White House chief usher in 1986.

GEORGE SULLIVAN

in charge of the servants whom some first families bring to the White House with them. John F. Kennedy had his own valet; the Johnsons, a cook; and the Nixons, a valet and a maid. When the Carters arrived, they brought a nursemaid for Amy. The Reagans relied exclusively on the regular staff.

Long before the first tourists begin lining up outside the East Gate, the White House staff has started work. The first employees arrive at six o'clock in the morning to begin the preparation of breakfast and the endless dusting, vacuuming, mopping, and polishing the rooms require.

Many of the employees work on rotating shifts. Those who begin at 6:00 A.M. work until 2:00 P.M. They are replaced by a shift that starts at 2:00 P.M. and continues until late in the evening, until after the first family has retired for the night.

Heavy cleaning is done by the housemen. A houseman waxes and buffs the floors. He vacuums the carpets.

Housemaids do the lighter cleaning. They change the bed linens on the second floor and dust and vacuum in each room, even the guest rooms not in use. "We never know when they will be used," says one employee.

After Harry Truman became president in 1945, following the death of Franklin Roosevelt, Mrs. Truman complained that the White House wasn't being kept as clean as the previous homes in which she had lived. Housekeeping, it seems, was not high on the list of Mrs. Roosevelt's many interests.

For a time, Mrs. Truman acted rather as an assistant housekeeper, often supervising the maids herself. She would stop a maid in the hall and say, "Could you take care of the fingerprints on the woodwork?" Mrs. Truman eventually replaced Mrs. Roosevelt's housekeeper with one of her own, and finally stopped giving instructions to the maids.

In his book, *Upstairs at the White House,* J. B. West recalled that the Trumans always treated the household help with respect—"respect for us personally, and respect for the work we did." If the president happened to be sitting in a room with a foreign dignitary, a prime minister, or a king, and a butler or a doorman entered the room, the president would introduce him. "They introduced all of their staff to their visitors," Mr. West noted.

While it was Mrs. Truman's ambition to get the woodwork to shine, Mrs. Eisenhower was concerned about footprints in the rugs. It bothered her that shoe marks showed on the thick carpets after people had walked on them. Whenever an important function was scheduled, Mrs. Eisenhower would order the rugs to be vacuumed again and again until no footprints showed. She even ordered special brushes, a separate brush for each color of rug. On the evening of a big event, after the butlers had dimmed the lights for the evening, the housemen would follow behind them, carefully brushing away their footprints.

Each piece of antique furniture in the White House is polished daily. The maids use lemon oil, not wax.

One man works full time washing windows. He is also in charge of the mansion's chandeliers. Each of the three chandeliers in the East Room takes two days to clean. The man sits on a scaffold beneath a chandelier and washes and polishes each piece of glass individually.

In the White House basement, there is a professionally equipped laundry. From early in the morning until late at night, one of the two White House laundresses is on duty there.

There are three White House doormen. They work in rotating shifts from the usher's office, which is just inside the front, or north, entrance to the Executive Mansion.

The doorman's chief responsibility is to greet guests, whether they be personal friends of the president or the first lady, or visiting heads of state.

The doorman operates the elevator used by the president

Washing White House windows is a full-time job.
THE WHITE HOUSE / BILL FITZ-PATRICK

and also delivers mail and messages meant for White House occupants. "He's our in-house mail system," says Mr. Walters.

At 12:30 in the afternoon, as soon as the last of the tourists has left, the ground floors start to hum with activity. Members of the operations staff take down the velvet ropes and stanchions used in guiding the tour groups. To prevent wear, certain rugs are removed each day before the tourists march through the rooms. These rugs have to be carried back inside and laid down again. That, too, is a job for the operations staff.

Carpets in each room visited by the tourists are vacuumed. Furniture and walls are dusted. The marble entrance and floor of the North Lobby are mopped and buffed. All brass is polished.

When the housemen and housemaids have completed work in a room, the executive housekeeper inspects it. She or he may plump the pillow on a sofa or adjust the position of a chair so that it sits in exactly the right spot.

By midafternoon, there is no trace of the several thousand visitors who paraded through the White House earlier in the day.

How does one get a job as a member of the White House's household staff? By applying to the chief usher.

But there are very few openings. The problem is that once someone is hired, he or she tends to remain in the job for years, for life, even. "I have to tell people who apply that we don't have a great deal of turnover," says Gary Walters. "In fact, when I became chief usher in 1986, there were still people on the staff who had been hired during Franklin Roosevelt's term of office."

Not only does a person have to satisfy the professional requirements for a job, but there is also the matter of security. The Secret Service does a thorough investigation of every candidate for a job. People who might otherwise be qualified are sometimes rejected because it is thought they might possibly jeopardize the safety of the president.

The first family's safety isn't the only consideration. There is also their privacy. People who work in the Executive Mansion see things and hear things that they must keep to themselves.

"When most people find out you work at the White House," says Gary Walters, "they want you to tell them something special that no one else knows. In fact, I think there is more curiosity about the White House and the first family today than ever before."

But the people on the household staff do nothing to satisfy the demands of the curious. They give no interviews. They seek no publicity. They write no articles or books. They are completely loyal to the presidency, to the man who happens to occupy the Oval Office, and to his family.

Those who work at the White House agree that their jobs provide some unusual benefits. "Each day is challenging and rewarding," says Gary Walters. "One of the most rewarding things is being able to learn what the families are like—without having to read about it in somebody's newspaper or hear it on television. You're able to make your own judgments."

There's also a certain excitement. You work in a house the entire world is watching. You are part of history in the making.

"I've worked here for seventeen years," said Gary Walters in 1987, "and I'm still excited about it. In fact, each day when I come through the gate, there's this little tingle of excitement I get. I guess when I lose that tingle, it will be time to leave."

4

Entertaining

In 1803, toward the end of his first term in office, Thomas Jefferson, in a letter to his daughter Martha, wrote:

> Four weeks from tomorrow, our winter campaign opens . . . the most serious trial I undergo. I wish much to turn it over to younger hands and to be myself but a guest at the table and free to leave it as others are.

The "winter campaign" that Jefferson spoke of had nothing to do with battlefield combat. He was referring to the White House social season.

Jefferson felt enormous pressure in carrying out the social obligations attached to being the nation's chief executive. Not only did the planning and preparation require an extraordinary amount of time, but such events were often critically important diplomatically. International relations could be deeply influenced by what was said over a beef roast or a glass of fine wine.

So it is today. In the case of official social functions, the president and first lady entertain on behalf of all Americans. They know they are making a lasting impression on the guest being honored. They do all they can to make it a very positive impression. Everything must be perfect, down to the smallest detail.

In planning social affairs, the first lady works closely with the chief usher and the executive chef. The first lady's social secretary also plays a key role.

The social secretary, who has her office in the East Wing, supervises a staff of about nine people. This is a far cry from the post of social secretary half a century ago, during the administration of Franklin Roosevelt. In those days, the social secretary worked only part-time. Edith Helm, the Roosevelts' social secretary, worked mornings, went home for lunch, and returned to the White House only if she had been asked to assist at afternoon teas.

In the case of important social events, Mrs. Helm's main responsibilities were to see to it that the invitations were correctly addressed and mailed, and keep track of those who accepted and those who didn't. She attended White House parties only when invited.

The duties and responsibilities of the social secretary mushroomed in importance when the Lyndon Johnsons named Bess Abell to take over the post. She had far more authority than any of her predecessors, not only in the case of private parties but also for official entertaining.

"She was in on everything," J. B. West, chief usher at the time, once noted. She handled the guest lists, told the chefs what to cook, dreamed up the decorations, and told the housekeeper not only what needed to be cleaned, but where to place the ashtrays.

Mrs. Gerald Ford supervises preparations for a state dinner in honor of President Alfonso Lopez Michelson of Colombia in September 1975.   GERALD R. FORD LIBRARY

Mrs. Abell was the first social secretary responsible for producing after-dinner entertainment in the East Room. She selected the guests who were to perform, directed rehearsals, and designed the program booklets. "Her instruction sheets were called scenarios," says J. B. West, "and the staff performed her instructions like actors on a Hollywood set."

Of course, Mrs. Abell's plans were approved by Lady Bird Johnson. Although Mrs. Johnson didn't get involved in the details, she had the final say on all of the important aspects of every social event.

Once a social function was underway, Mrs. Abell acted as an assistant hostess, mixing with the guests, making introductions, and starting conversations.

The social secretaries who have followed Mrs. Abell have

A ballet company performs in the East Room following a
state dinner at the Johnson White House in 1968.

maintained the role as she fashioned it. But they have always
remained in the background, giving the first lady the credit for
any success they might have achieved. Muffie Brandon, social
secretary for Nancy Reagan, had this to say about her boss:
"Mrs. Reagan's involvement is direct. She oversees the guest
list, the flowers, the wines, the entertainment—everything."

Entertaining can take the form of a simple reception, a
music or dance recital, a breakfast for lawmakers, or an outdoor barbecue. Dwight Eisenhower, who liked to cook, sometimes invited friends to a cookout on the White House roof,
where he broiled steaks on a charcoal grill.

There are White House parties to celebrate the Fourth of
July and Christmas. The Fords invited more than nine hun-

dred guests to a Christmas party for members of Congress in 1974. Parties are also given when the president wants to celebrate a legislative victory in Congress.

In November 1981, Mrs. Reagan introduced a new concert series to entertain White House guests. Called "Young Artists in Performance at the White House," the series featured musicians of exceptional skill and their famous sponsors. The performances were taped and shown on national television.

In the case of small dinners for friends, the Reagans liked to entertain by showing a film in the White House movie theater. The president always asked the kitchen to prepare popcorn for such occasions.

Year in and year out, the most important functions on the White House social calendar are the dinners given to honor visiting royalty or heads of state. Such dinners require an enormous amount of planning and effort, with virtually everyone on the White House staff playing a role.

The planning begins many months in advance, when diplomatic representatives set the date for the dinner. A theme for the dinner is then chosen to fit the national culture and personal tastes of the guests being honored. This is often reflected in the musical entertainment. For example, when President and Mrs. Sandro Pertini of Italy were being honored by the Reagans, two well-known singers of Italian descent—Frank Sinatra and Perry Como—were chosen to entertain.

One of the most celebrated state dinners in recent years took place in December 1987, when Soviet leader Mikhail Gorbachev and his wife were the honored guests. After-dinner entertainment was provided by pianist Van Cliburn who, in 1958, became the first American to win the Tchaikovsky competition in Moscow. Van Cliburn was well known to the

Soviet leader Mikhail Gorbachev warmly
embraces pianist Van Cliburn after a performance at a White House state dinner in
1987.   WIDE WORLD

Gorbachevs, who thoroughly enjoyed his performance and
hailed him with loud applause.

World-famous ballet dancers and opera stars perform, too.
In recent years, White House guests have been entertained by
the cast of the Broadway musical *A Chorus Line,* members of
the Harlem Ballet, and the Juilliard String Quartet.

People invited to such dinners include cabinet secretaries, members of Congress, industrialists, Nobel Prize winners, fashion designers, artists, authors, publishers, and editors. During Ronald Reagan's term of office, guests also included several of the Reagans' Hollywood pals, such as Bob Hope, Charlton Heston, and Audrey Hepburn.

Of course, the guest list takes into consideration the particular head of state being honored. When Chinese President Li Xiannian and Madame Li were guests, architect I. M. Pei, author Bette Bao Lord, and choreographer Choo San Goh were among the guests invited.

Each person on the guest list receives a small, stiff white envelope containing an invitation. In handsome script prepared by an expert calligrapher, the invitation begins: "The President and Mrs. Reagan request the pleasure of . . ." The guest's name appears in the same highly decorative handwriting, or calligraphy. (There are four calligraphers on the White House Staff.)

A small card enclosed with the invitation explains the purpose of the evening. Other enclosures are a response card and an admit card.

The names of possible guests for each dinner are submitted by senior White House staff members. The first lady and her aides go over the lists carefully, rejecting some names, adding others.

Nancy Reagan not only approved the guest list for state dinners but also the decorations, entertainment, and menu. In an effort to help assure the success of the meal, Mrs. Reagan had the executive chef prepare a tryout meal about a week before the event. As Mrs. Reagan sampled the dishes, she took notes, and later met with the chef and offered suggestions she thought might improve the meal.

Nancy Reagan liked to have each dinner's menu printed in "Franglaise," a blend of French and English. At a state dinner for Chancellor Helmut Schmidt of West Germany, the various courses included smoked mountain trout, roast supreme of duckling a l'orange with wild rice and raisins, watercress and mushroom salad, Brie and Chevre cheeses, and melon glace en surprise.

The day before the dinner, the White House staff has much to do. As soon as the tours have ended, thirteen round tables are wheeled into the State Dining Room and places for ten are set at each.

After the table covers and cloths are in place, maids iron out every wrinkle. Then one table is completely set as a model for the others. The place settings include china, silver, water glasses, wine glasses and champagne glasses. Each also includes a menu card, and a small card with the guest's name, prepared by a White House calligrapher.

The 130 guests require 1,040 pieces of table china, 1,040 knives, forks, and spoons, and 520 crystal goblets.

At the same time the State Dining Room is being readied, the East Room, where the entertainment is to be offered, is undergoing a similar transformation. A stage is installed. Potted shrubs and trees are carted in for decoration. At the North Portico, where the president will greet his honored guests, red carpeting is laid down.

Meanwhile, the kitchen is bustling with activity. An extra chef and a cook or two have been brought in from outside to assist the regular staff.

On the evening of the dinner, everything unfolds on a carefully planned schedule. The guests arrive at the East Gate. Each turns over to the guard an admittance card sent out a few

A White House butler arranges silverware before a state
dinner in 1975.   GERALD R. FORD LIBRARY

days earlier. Guards scan the cards beneath ultraviolet light to
assure each is genuine. Then each guest is escorted into the
White House.

The guests follow the same route covered by tourists, past
the library, Vermeil Room, China Room, and the Diplomatic
Reception Room, and then upstairs to the North Entrance
Hall.

At the top of the stairs, the doorman awaits them. He stands
behind a small table. As the guests come forward, the doorman
checks each person's name from a list before him. He hands
each guest a small white envelope that contains the number
of the table at which the guest is to be seated.

The guests enter the East Room to await the president, who
has already greeted the visiting head of state and his or her
spouse. As the presidential party, led by a military honor

guard, descends the grand stairway from the family floor and enters the East Room, drums salute the honored guest with "Ruffles and Flourishes." Then the Marine Orchestra strikes up "Hail to the Chief." The guests applaud. Members of the presidential party then greet each of the guests.

It takes about a half hour for the guests to go through the receiving line. Then the guests proceed down the long, red-carpeted hallway to the State Dining Room. An honor guard is posted on each side of the hallway. The president, the first lady, and their guests are the last to enter the dining room.

Once the meal is served, guests take their dining cues from the president, who is served first. No one touches a fork or spoon until the president begins to eat. President Calvin Coolidge once used this custom to play a joke on his guests. Toward the end of the meal, Coolidge carefully poured his coffee and some cream into a saucer. Several guests politely did the same. Then, as they waited for Coolidge to take a sip, the president smiled slightly, leaned over, and put the saucer on the floor for his cat.

By 9:30 P.M., the meal is over and the butlers have removed the china. It is time for the exchange of toasts by the two heads of state, a time for saluting common ties and the achievements of allies.

After dinner, the guests gather in the Red, Green, and Blue Rooms, where coffee and liqueurs are served. As souvenirs, most guests take their menu cards and place cards. They also take White House matchbooks.

By now, the evening is much less formal. It is time to relax and perhaps chat with a motion-picture star, a sports head-liner, a Supreme Court justice, a senator, or perhaps even a head of state.

When the after-dinner reception is over, the guests go back

Guests dine as strolling violinists play at a state dinner given
by President and Mrs. Lyndon Johnson in 1967.

LYNDON BAINES JOHNSON LIBRARY

to the East Room. Gilt chairs have been arranged in semicircu-
lar rows for entertainment.

The entertainment lasts about forty minutes. While the
guests are enjoying it, the White House staff is preparing for
the dancing that is to follow. Chairs and small tables with
flowers and candles are placed in the Cross Hall between the
East Room and the State Dining Room. Music for the dancing
is provided by the Marine Orchestra, which has been pared
down to dance-band size.

At the same time as the Cross Hall is being readied for
dancing, the chairs and all but three or four of the big circular
tables are being removed from the State Dining Room, where
champagne is to be served later. Each piece of china, glass-

51

ware, and flatware is washed by hand. Extra dishwashers have been brought in to help out.

Everything is packed into big crates. Then the crates are taken down to the basement to be stored until the next dinner.

"With all the furniture moving and other activity, it's like backstage at a play," says Chief Usher Gary J. Walters. "Yet the guests have no idea of all that's going on."

The president and first lady dance, too. During the time Lyndon Johnson served as president, social functions usually put emphasis on dancing. President Johnson danced with many of the women present and often selected dancing partners for his guests.

The Fords also enjoyed dancing a great deal. "I dance with anyone who asks me," Mrs. Ford once told an interviewer. "My husband does, too. Some of the women ask, 'Mr. President, may I have this dance?'—and it's all right, because we try to keep the evening as informal as possible."

The end of the evening is signaled when the president and the first lady escort their guests to the North Portico. There they say their farewells and the guests depart.

Although dancing may continue until almost midnight, the formal part of the evening is over.

The White House staff still has much to do, however. The Executive Mansion has to be put in readiness for the tour groups, which begin arriving early the next morning. The chairs and stage have to be removed from the East Room and put back into storage. Carpets have to be rolled up and removed. Floors have to be polished again.

By this time, the president and his wife are probably asleep. "We have to be very careful about the noise level," says Gary Walters. "Sometimes we wait until the next morning—before the tours—to do the moving."

During Lyndon Johnson's term in office, social functions often stressed dancing. Here, President Johnson dances with Great Britain's Princess Margaret.

Long after the last guests have departed, lights continue to glow on the first and ground floors of the Executive Mansion, as work continues. The china, crystal, and silver must be washed, dried, and polished. It may be 2:00 or 3:00 A.M. before the last piece is back in storage.

As the day is winding down, the key figures in the operation of the White House are thinking about the next day. The chief usher, who must be on duty early the next morning, makes use of the daybed in his first-floor office, and sleeps overnight. The executive chef, who also has a bed in his office, sleeps over too.

The streams of tourists will be arriving soon. There will be meals to be prepared and served, dishes to be washed, and floors to be polished. The president may be hosting a luncheon, or perhaps it will be the first lady who is doing the entertaining.

For the people behind the scenes, it will be another day of serving the president, making it as easy as possible for him and his family to live and work in the White House.

5

From the Kitchen

It was Monday, January 20, 1969, the first day of the administration of Richard Nixon. The household staff was tense, as they are whenever a new president takes over.

What new demands were going to be made upon them? What new standards of taste and style were going to be imposed? It was a time of uncertainty for the staff.

In preparation for the new White House occupants, Executive Chef Henry Haller laid in supplies for weeks, trying to buy everything the Nixons liked. "We could have opened a grocery store in the pantry," he said.

That evening, in her first call to Chef Haller, Mrs. Nixon ordered dinner for the first family. "Tricia and Julie [the Nixons' daughters] and the president would like steak for dinner in the upstairs dining room," said Mrs. Nixon. "And I'd like a bowl of cottage cheese in my bedroom."

The steaks were no problem. Chef Haller had heard that the Nixon family loved steak, and he had several fresh, juicy tenderloins on hand.

But cottage cheese? There was not a spoonful of cottage cheese in all of the White House.

Chef Haller requested a White House limousine. Then he asked the head butler to take the limousine and speed around downtown Washington until he found a store where cottage cheese could be purchased.

The mission was successful. Mrs. Nixon was able to enjoy her cottage cheese that evening, without realizing the panic she had caused in the kitchen. Chef Haller was never without cottage cheese again.

Being executive chef in the White House means having to cope with first families who like unusual foods or have curious eating habits. Mrs. Nixon and her craving for cottage cheese is only one example. President Lyndon Johnson, a rapid eater, liked his salad chopped so fine he could eat it with a spoon. Johnson, who was from Texas, enjoyed such specialities as black-eyed peas, deer sausage, and barbecued ribs.

The Fords gave evidence of their midwestern roots by requesting German apple pancakes, red cabbage, and lemon-sponge pudding.

Early presidents, too, had their favorite foods. Andrew Jackson found turkey hash hard to resist. George Washington relished cream of peanut soup and sweet potatoes sprinkled with coconut.

Special foods are only part of the problem. The White House chef must also be ready to meet demands that could be considered unreasonable. President Jimmy Carter once asked Chef Haller to put together a dinner for 1,300 people on the White House lawn to celebrate the Camp David Accords, an important document in the Middle East peace process. The hitch was that the president gave Mr. Haller only a week in

These tents were erected when President Jimmy Carter ordered a dinner for 1,300 people on the White House lawn to celebrate the signing of the Camp David Accords.

which to do it. Mary Hoyt, press secretary to Mrs. Carter, called the experience a nightmare. To Mr. Haller, it was a "shocker."

The executive chef has to learn to remain calm, no matter what. During Mr. Haller's tenure, the king of Saudi Arabia once arrived for a White House visit with his own food in five briefcases and his own food taster.

As any chef who has filled the role can testify, working in the White House is no easy job. The kitchen staff is expected to provide food for all official dinners, receptions, luncheons, teas, and conferences—and for the members of the first family as well. If there is a need for Danish pastry and coffee for thirty early morning guests, the White House doesn't call a Washington bakery. The pastry chef makes the Danish.

The hours are very long. The day often begins at 6:00 A.M. or so and stretches until after midnight.

The staff is not big when compared to that of most large restaurants or hotel kitchens. It consists of only four other chefs, including the pastry chef. The kitchen can get very frantic. Once, during the Bicentennial celebration in 1976, the White House held seven state dinners in six weeks. One of the guests of honor was Queen Elizabeth II of England.

Henry Haller, from Altdorf, Switzerland, who came to the United States after World War II, is perhaps the most noted of all White House executive chefs. His twenty-one-year tour of duty covered five administrations, during which time he was responsible for the preparation of more than 250 state dinners. Mr. Haller left the White House in 1987 at the age of sixty-five.

Mr. Haller was the executive chef at the Hampshire House in New York City when he was asked to take over at the White House. Lyndon Johnson was president at the time. As vice president, Mr. Johnson had once stayed at the Hampshire House and enjoyed the food there. He recommended Mr. Haller for the job.

The Eisenhowers were the first presidential family to employ a professionally trained chef. Before that, navy stewards were responsible for preparing and serving White House family meals and official entertaining.

After Henry Haller left the post of executive chef late in 1987, Jon Hill, who had worked for a major hotel chain, was named to replace him. The next year, Hans Raffert, formerly an assistant chef under Henry Haller, succeeded Chef Hill.

White House executive chefs were aided by pastry chef Roland Mesnier, from France. Chef Mesnier began working at the White House during the administration of Jimmy Carter.

58

Chef Haller examines an elegant lobster salad as preparation work goes on in the background.　　　WIDE WORLD

He was once hailed by the *New York Times* as a "sculptor of sugar, a carver of chocolate and a master of marzipan." He prepared some two to three hundred different desserts for White House functions during the Carter and Reagan administrations.

Chef Mesnier was often praised for his creativity. "If he served raspberry sherbert thirty days in a row," Assistant Chef Frank Ruda once said of him, "he'd serve it thirty different ways."

Mesnier's creations included a dessert of tiny balls of chocolate mint sherbert that were set in cookie shells shaped like leaves. Each leaf had veins of chocolate.

President Reagan, who had a sweet tooth, often asked for

Jon Hill took over as White House executive chef in 1987. WIDE WORLD

second helpings of Mesnier's desserts. On weekends when the Reagans went to Camp David, the president sometimes asked for a supply of Mesnier's cookies to take with him.

Another of the White House chefs is assigned to prepare meals for the first family. He or she works out of a separate kitchen on the second floor of the Executive Mansion.

The first family must pay for the groceries that are purchased for private meals. But no one has to go shopping at the supermarket. All food is purchased at wholesalers that have been granted special Secret Service clearance. In addition, only selected people at each of the wholesalers are permitted to handle food meant for the first family's dinner table. When the White House order is ready, it is picked up by Secret Service agents.

The Reagans' attitude toward food and dining was fairly typical of that of modern-day presidents. Concerned about their waistlines, they restrained themselves at mealtime.

Most of the nation's early presidents, on the other hand, gave free rein to their appetites. When Ulysses S. Grant was president, during the 1870s, White House banquets sometimes consisted of as many as twenty-nine courses. About halfway through, a frozen punch was served. (State dinners today normally have four courses—an appetizer; soup; the main course, or entree; and dessert.)

Overeating at holiday time was a tradition. John and Abigail Adams, for example, called one of their Christmas Day dinners "A Most Sinful Feast." Besides the roast turkey, the menu included baked ham and boiled beef. There were eight desserts. A Reagan Christmas Day menu was simple by comparison.

During the week, the Reagans often had breakfast together, dining on fruit and cold cereal or soft-boiled eggs and decaffeinated coffee. Mrs. Reagan frequently had lunch at her desk in an office sitting room down the hall from her bedroom. Soup and a salad were what she usually ordered for lunch.

The president usually had lunch in the Oval Office. But occasionally he would order it to be served in the family quar-

THE JOHN ADAMS CHRISTMAS DAY MENU

Crab Claws with Dill-Mustard Sauce
Winter Squash Soup
Poached Salmon with Egg Sauce
Native Roasted Turkey with Sausage and Sage Dressing
Baked Ham from the Smokehouse
Beef Bouilli with Horseradish Sauce
Yams and Chestnuts Baked with Pippins
Mrs. Boylston's Asparagus
Carrot Pudding
Mess of Peas
Skillet Cranberries for a Slack Oven
Watermelon Pickle
Madeira Wine Jelly Garnished with Frosted Fruit
Crane House Pumpkin Bread
Braintree Squash Rolls
Oyster Rolls
Floating Island, or Snow Eggs
Brandied Nectarines
Currant Pound Cake
Coffee or Tea
Candied Ginger
Spiced Pecans
Whiskey Nut Balls
Candied Peel
Angelica Stems
Cluster Raisins

Turkey with Chestnut and Wild Mushroom Dressing
Giblet Gravy
Baby Carrots with Cranberry Glaze
Broccoli Christmas Tree with Turnip Ornaments
Monkey Bread
Red and Green Salad with Pine and Sesame Dressing
Little Snowmen of Coconut Ice Cream
on Winter Wonderland Scene of Spun Sugar
Snowflake Cookies

ters upstairs. It was always very simple, frequently soup and half a grapefruit.

The Reagans' evening meal was usually made up of fish, chicken, or veal with fresh vegetables and a salad of some kind. Once in a while, Mr. Reagan would order one of his favorites, such as lasagne or macaroni and cheese. Often, the Reagans ate from trays in the president's study. While dining, the president and Mrs. Reagan did what millions of Americans do: They watched the evening news on television.

Once a meal has been prepared, it is taken by butlers to be served. The White House staff includes six butlers. In the case of state dinners or other functions where a large number of guests are on hand, extra butlers are brought in.

The Reagans often had their evening meal served on trays in front of the television.   THE WHITE HOUSE / MICHAEL EVANS

The butlers are supervised by the maitre d', another key figure in the operation of the White House. John Ficklin, who served nine presidents, was a White House fixture for forty-four years, about half of them as maitre d'. He was frequently the first person the presidents and first ladies saw in the morning and sometimes the last person they saw before going to bed. Mr. Ficklin retired during Ronald Reagan's first administration.

Mr. Ficklin began working at the White House in 1939 as a part-time pantry man, washing dishes and shining the silver for luncheons, dinners, and receptions. His first day on the job, he met the president. Mr. Ficklin and a coworker were carrying large ornamental branched candlesticks into the elevator. In the elevator, seated in his wheelchair, was Franklin D. Roosevelt.

"Welcome aboard," Mr. Roosevelt said to the astonished young men. Then the president introduced himself.

In the years that followed, Mr. Ficklin had an opportunity to see presidents and their families as real people, not as press secretaries or other image makers necessarily wanted them to be seen.

Harry and Bess Truman, Mr. Ficklin once recalled, treated him as one of the family. Mr. Ficklin, then a butler, served the Trumans breakfast each morning. That was the time of day the Trumans always inquired about the members of the household staff. Charles Ficklin, John's brother, was also a member of the staff. One day, Charles was ill and unable to report for work. Mrs. Truman wanted to know where Charles was. When she learned that Charles was not feeling well, Mrs. Truman asked the White House physician to look at him. The physician reported that Charles had pneumonia and should be hospitalized.

When Charles was in the hospital, Harry Truman sneaked out of the White House to see him. "He walked up the back steps and right into the room," Mr. Ficklin said. "There were no nurses, no doctors, nobody in there but my brother and the president."

While a butler usually serves food, the job actually involves a great deal more than that. "You just can't put down on paper everything a butler would do," Mr. Ficklin said. "Instead of calling someone and saying the president or first lady wants such and such, you'd just go and do it yourself."

Workdays often lasted from breakfast straight through to midnight, if there happened to be a state dinner. It was not until the Eisenhower administration that Mr. Ficklin and other butlers began to be paid for working overtime. It was

Mrs. Gerald Ford says farewell to maitre d' John Ficklin not long before the Fords' final departure from the White House in 1977.   GERALD R. FORD LIBRARY

also under Mr. Eisenhower that Mr. Ficklin was advanced to the position of head butler.

Mr. Ficklin remembered the day that President John F. Kennedy was assassinated, and the sadness and pain that gripped the White House staff. "The night before the funeral," Mr. Ficklin said, "we were preparing to feed all those kings, presidents, and prime ministers, when Mr. West [J. B. West, the chief usher] told me that Mrs. Kennedy wanted me to be an usher at the church." Mr. Ficklin's first reaction was to say no. But he knew it was an honor to be asked. Besides, he was eager to do whatever Mrs. Kennedy wanted him to do. Then a problem developed. He didn't have a morning suit, the formal apparel that ushers were to wear. That was solved by getting the owner of a retail store out of bed to alter a suit for Mr. Ficklin to wear the next morning.

From the Kitchen

It was during the Johnson administration that Mr. Ficklin became the White House maitre d'. One of his duties was to escort the president to his seat at state dinners.

During his years at the White House, Mr. Ficklin served at many hundreds of state dinners. At the last state dinner he attended, in 1982, he got to sit down as a guest. The dinner was held in honor of the amir of Bahrain. Mr. Ficklin had just announced his retirement, and Nancy Reagan invited him to be her guest and sit at her table.

—6—
Sports and Recreation

Late at night, when the bowling league of White House employees had finished playing, President Richard Nixon sometimes used to steal away to the lanes and roll a few games. "You could never tell when he was going to come down," Joe Taylor, caretaker of the lanes, once recalled. "And you never knew who was coming with him. Normally he liked to bowl by himself."

Nixon would bowl one game after another in rapid succession, sometimes as many as twenty games in one evening. He holds the presidential high score of 233.

Lady Bird Johnson, the wife of President Lyndon Johnson, was an excellent bowler, too. She once chalked up a score of 188.

Mrs. Johnson used to invite the wives of cabinet members to bowl. Or sometimes she would be joined by her daughter Lynda for a friendly game or two. Muriel Humphrey, wife of Vice President Hubert Humphrey, was another of Mrs. Johnson's bowling companions.

"She really loved to bowl," Joe Taylor said of Mrs. Johnson.

"Once in a while she'd have him [President Johnson] come over."

Through the years the presidents and their families have taken part in a wide range of sports and leisure-time activities. Bowling is merely one of them. Through these recreational pursuits, they have sought to relax, keep fit, or simply enjoy themselves.

In her book, *White House Diary,* Mrs. Johnson told how she sometimes used bowling to reduce the pressures of White House life. Mrs. Johnson described events during a crisis in the Mideast on June 5, 1967, in these words: "The U.N. was struggling . . . the Security Council going into session for five or six hours . . . like millions of others I strained with hope toward the U.N. and what it might produce. But I remembered with dismay the expressions of no confidence. . . .

"I turned off the TV and went over to the bowling lanes, where I used up my energy in three games, hurling a heavier ball than usual and running up scores in the 150s. All by myself. And while I'm bowling, I don't think about anything else."

During Jimmy Carter's administration, the president's daughter, Amy, who was nine years old when the Carters moved into the White House, used to bowl with friends. But Ronald Reagan and the members of his family were not bowlers. Mr. Taylor, in fact, never saw Mr. Reagan bowl.

That doesn't mean that the lanes weren't used. The White House has an eight-team bowling league composed of the employees, including the Uniformed Division of the Secret Service. The lanes get plenty of use.

Two bowling lanes were presented to Harry Truman in 1947, a gift from the people of his home state of Missouri. They were placed in the basement of the West Wing. But since the

President Harry Truman (without bowling shoes) delivers the ball at the formal opening of the White House bowling lanes on April 19, 1947.   WIDE WORLD

clatter of crashing pins sometimes intruded on White House conversations, the lanes were moved next door to the Old Executive Office Building in 1955.

The Nixons, who took up residence in the White House in 1969, found it inconvenient to walk next door to the Old Executive Office Building to bowl. So Mr. Nixon arranged for a one-lane bowling alley to be installed underneath the driveway leading to the North Portico in an area where the carpentry shop and other workspaces were to be found.

Not only did Mr. and Mrs. Nixon use the lane, but the Nixons' daughters and sons-in-law found enjoyment and exercise there. It is still available to members of the first family and their friends.

Bowling, of course, is only one of the recreational activities available to White House occupants. For the sports-minded president, there's much to do there. There is a tennis court, a heated outdoor swimming pool, and a game room with billiards and Ping-Pong.

The White House theater, which seats sixty-five, is supplied with the latest films as well as presidential favorites. There's a library that offers more than 2,700 volumes, the best works by hundreds of American authors.

The swimming pool is taken for granted nowadays, but early presidents who enjoyed taking a dip had to get along without one. This didn't bother them very much, however. John Quincy Adams often swam in the Potomac River, about a mile's walk from the White House.

Adams was president during the 1820s, a time when men sometimes went swimming without clothing. Adams followed this custom. He simply folded his shirt, pantaloons, and underclothing and left them on the riverbank.

Pat and Richard Nixon, both avid bowlers,
arranged for the installation of a private
White House lane.
WOMEN'S INTERNATIONAL BOWLING CONGRESS

Theodore Roosevelt, who served from 1901 to 1909, is another president who is known to have enjoyed nude swims in the Potomac. But on other occasions, Roosevelt didn't bother to disrobe. He would place his watch and money in his hat, set the hat aside, and plunge in fully clothed. "What difference does it make?" he once asked. "It's the shortest, quickest way, and a wetting does no harm."

Teddy Roosevelt is believed to be the last president to have swum, clothed or otherwise, in the Potomac. The first White House pool dates to the administration of Franklin D. Roosevelt.

In 1921, when he was thirty-nine, Roosevelt suffered an attack of poliomyelitis, which cost him the use of his legs. Afterward, he found great joy in swimming, using his powerful arms and shoulders to propel himself through the water.

Not long after Roosevelt became president in 1933, the New York *Daily News* asked permission of the president and Congress to embark on a fund-raising campaign for a White House swimming pool. Once permission was granted, it didn't take long to collect the $40,000 necessary to build the pool. Part of the money came from pennies collected from schoolchildren.

Roosevelt used the pool, which could be heated for year-round use, almost every evening. He would quit work about five-thirty to take an hour-long swim before dinner. Although he could not use his paralyzed legs, his arm, shoulder, and back muscles were well developed; he could outswim just about every member of his staff.

Harry Truman, who became president upon Roosevelt's death, referred to the White House pool as his "swimming hole." Truman, whose specialty was the sidestroke, always swam with his head above the water to avoid getting his glasses wet.

Dwight Eisenhower, who replaced Truman in the Oval Office, seldom used the swimming pool during the early part of his administration. But after Eisenhower suffered a heart attack, his doctors recommended swimming as part of his rehabilitation program. The presidential swim, thirty minutes in length, was scheduled at noon each day, with the water temperature at 85 to 90 degrees Fahrenheit.

John Kennedy used the pool for reasons of health, too. Kennedy's problem was a bad back. He swam twenty to thirty minutes before lunch and again in the early evening, with the pool heated to 90 degrees. The regimen eased the back pain which plagued Kennedy almost constantly. Kennedy also performed special exercises each day to strengthen his back muscles.

Often Kennedy swam with Dave Powers, a member of his staff. Powers once informed newsmen that there was one important rule to be observed while swimming with the president. "You've got to keep your head above the water so you can talk," said Powers.

Lyndon Johnson swam regularly in the White House pool. Richard Nixon used it only occasionally.

During Nixon's first term, the swimming pool fell victim to alterations that were made in the West Wing of the White House. Mr. Nixon turned the West Wing press lobby into a reception lounge. He then ordered beams to be laid across the swimming pool and facilities for the press to be built on top.

But the White House was not without a swimming pool for very long. After Gerald Ford replaced Mr. Nixon in the sum-

Lyndon Johnson *(right)* enjoys a swim with aides Lloyd Hand
(left) and Jack Valenti in the White House indoor pool.

mer of 1974, he began to look for a site for an outdoor pool on
the White House grounds. It was not as simple as finding an
area of the right dimensions and saying, "Let's put it there."
Any construction involving the White House and its grounds
must be approved by several different organizations. These
include the Secret Service, which advises on the safety of the
site; the National Park Service, which has responsibility for the
grounds; the National Fine Arts Commission, which advises on
architectural changes in historic areas of the nation's capitol;
and the Committee for the Preservation of the White House.
As one observer told the *Washington Post:* "It would be easier
to move the Washington Monument to Connecticut Avenue
and K Street than to build a swimming pool in the backyard
of the White House."

Gerald Ford attracts reporters at the opening of the outdoor swimming pool.   GERALD R. FORD LIBRARY

The following year, 1975, all of the interested parties handed down their decision. They agreed upon a site that was about 60 feet south of the West Wing in a spot formerly occupied by dog kennels.

Construction of the pool was completed by mid-July 1975. It is 22 feet wide, almost 55 feet long, and 9 feet deep at its deepest point. It is fitted out with a 10-foot diving board. The president can get to the pool through the White House basement by means of an underground tunnel with a stairway at the end that leads to within a foot of the pool's edge.

As soon as the pool was filled for the first time, President Ford began using it. And, whenever the weather permitted, daily dips were a part of Mr. Ford's schedule.

One of the most athletic presidents, Mr. Ford enjoyed tennis, too. GERALD R. FORD LIBRARY

For well over half a century, presidents have also been
able to enjoy tennis on the White House court, which is located on the South Lawn west of the large, circular fountain.
Trees and thick shrubbery conceal the court from the view
of tourists and passersby.

Among recent presidents, both Gerald Ford and Jimmy
Carter were avid tennis players and used the court often.
While Ronald Reagan shunned tennis, his vice president,
George Bush, made use of the court whenever he could. "Visitors love playing there, and it's easy for me to change into my
tennis gear there," Mr. Bush once told *Tennis* magazine. "The
setting, especially in the spring with the tulips in bloom, ranks
right up there at the top."

President Jimmy Carter changes sides and has a few words
with Hamilton Jordan, a top aide. JIMMY CARTER LIBRARY

Theodore Roosevelt, besides enjoying swimming, was another tennis-playing president. In fact, it was Roosevelt who
installed the first White House tennis court, and he had it built
right outside his office. He could practically step from the office
onto the court.

Roosevelt used the court whenever possible, even on Washington's hottest, most humid days, or when the court was so
rain-soaked the ball scarcely bounced. Diplomats and other
official visitors who had appointments with the president
sometimes had to wait until Roosevelt finished an exciting
match.

For his opponents, Roosevelt chose from among a group of
young government officials. Some of these players became

Roosevelt's close friends and advisers. Newspapers of the day sometimes referred to these gentlemen as Roosevelt's Tennis Cabinet.

In the fall of 1909, toward the end of Roosevelt's administration, the tennis court was removed to make way for an expansion of office space. The new court was constructed in the spring of 1910. By the time it was completed, William Howard Taft, a golfer, not a tennis player, was president.

Besides tennis, swimming, and bowling, presidents have taken part in a wide range of other physical pursuits. Benjamin Harrison purchased a rowing machine that provided pleasant exercise. A brochure advertising the machine is preserved among Harrison's papers.

For Herbert Hoover, the sport was medicine ball. Every morning except Sunday, at seven o'clock, Hoover, his cabinet officers, and several aides would gather on the White House lawn, and for half an hour or so would toss the cumbersome eight-pound ball over a high net.

Following the game, a light breakfast would be served outdoors. The president and other ballplayers, sometimes wrapped in heavy blankets, would enjoy grapefruit, toast, and coffee while chatting amicably.

One reason Hoover liked the sport was because it helped him control his weight. "It required less skill than tennis," he wrote in his *Memoirs,* "was faster and more vigorous, and therefore gave more exercise in a short time."

Harry Truman's favorite sport was horseshoes. After he became president, he ordered the construction of a horseshoe pitching court. He frequently invited close friends to join him in games.

Ronald Reagan enjoyed outdoor exercise—horseback ri-

Hoover's aides and cabinet officers would gather on the White House South Lawn every day except Sunday to toss around a medicine ball. HERBERT HOOVER LIBRARY

ding and firewood chopping, hauling, and stacking. These were activities he pursued at his ranch in the Santa Ynez Mountains of California.

As Mr. Reagan once noted in *Parade* magazine, "There is not a lot of wood to chop or trails to clear on the White House lawn." To keep fit during the years he occupied the Executive Mansion, Mr. Reagan had a gym set up on the second floor. It was equipped with a weight scale, an exercise bicycle, and a machine with pulleys and weights that enabled him to do a variety of exercises for the arms, shoulders, legs, and belly. There was also a treadmill, a continuously moving belt on which the president walked fast or jogged.

Mr. Reagan's workout program began with ten minutes of

warm-up calisthenics followed by about fifteen minutes of work on the machines. "I have two different sets of exercises I do on alternate days," he told *Parade*. "Each exercise is for specific muscles."

So his exercise program wouldn't become boring, Mr. Reagan varied the drills and kept them brief. He also had a few other tricks. For instance, he had a television screen mounted in front of the treadmill. As he walked, he watched newscasts.

Presidential sports have not always been strenuous ones. There's billiards, for instance. A game similar to pool that is played on an enclosed, cloth-covered table with hard balls and a cue, billiards has been available in the White House since the 1820s.

President John Quincy Adams ordered the purchase of the first White House billiard table. Although it cost only sixty-one dollars, the purchase of the table was attacked by the president's political enemies as a terrible waste of public money. The criticism was so heated and persistent that two of Adams's supporters in Congress had to defend the expenditure on the floor of the House of Representatives. In the end, Adams paid for the table out of his own pocket.

Ulysses S. Grant was another billiards enthusiast. Grant had a separate billiards room built, and he and his White House guests would often go there after dinner to puff on cigars and attempt difficult shots.

When Rutherford B. Hayes succeeded Grant, billiards fell upon dismal days. Lucy Hayes, the president's wife, who had banned the serving of liquor in the White House (for which she earned the nickname Lemonade Lucy), decided that billiards was not a game for the president. She ordered the billiard table moved to the basement.

Billiards remained out of fashion at the White House until

the first administration of Woodrow Wilson. World War I was raging at the time. Mrs. Wilson, anxious to find ways to relieve the pressures on her husband, thought billiards might serve that purpose. She had a billiards room fitted out on the ground floor of the Executive Mansion.

Mrs. Wilson's idea was a good one. The president came to relish the game. He even taught his daughters how to play.

For modern-day presidents, billiards is available in the White House game room on the third floor. But the game has never come close to achieving the popularity it enjoyed during the Adams, Grant, and Wilson administrations.

No discussion of White House sports and recreation would be complete without mentioning golf, a sport enjoyed by most twentieth-century presidents. Although he was bothered by a bad back, John F. Kennedy was perhaps the best golfer to occupy the White House. Fred Corcoran of the Professional Golfers Association once said of him: "If there were a match among the five presidents who played golf, Kennedy would win, Eisenhower would finish second about four strokes behind him, and Wilson, Harding, and Taft would all have trouble breaking 100."

As a college player at Harvard, Kennedy shot in the seventies. In later life, he usually finished in the eighties.

Kennedy took advantage of the spacious White House South Lawn to practice his golf shots. He would place a doormat on the grass. Then, using a seven-, eight-, or nine-iron, he would hit one high-arching pitch shot after another.

Warren Harding used the lawn as a golf range, too. He drove balls from a carpet he spread on the turf. Often the president's dog, Laddie Boy, would be sent to retrieve Harding's drives.

Dwight Eisenhower is rated as one of the best of the golfing
presidents.　　　　　　　DWIGHT D. EISENHOWER LIBRARY

To Harding and Kennedy, Wilson and Taft, golf was a sport
to be enjoyed as a leisure-time activity. But Dwight Eisenhower was almost fanatical about the game. The White House
grounds came to reflect this passion.

Although he first played the game in 1927, Eisenhower did

not become a serious player until after World War II. He worked hard to sharpen his skills. He practiced diligently. He took lessons.

As president, Eisenhower usually played on Wednesdays and Saturdays at Burning Tree Country Club in Virginia. There he worked with Ed Dudley, the pro, on improving his game.

Not long after his inauguration in 1953, Eisenhower took one look at the vast open spaces offered by the South Lawn and decided it would be excellent for golf practice. He began hitting pitch shots whenever he had a chance, targeting an imaginary green. He assigned his valet to shag balls for him.

It wasn't long before curious spectators began to gather at the fence to watch. Sometimes motorists even left their cars to run up to the fence and take a look or snap a picture. When the crowd got too big, Eisenhower would retreat to his office.

Eventually Eisenhower developed a special routine for practice on the South Lawn. Whenever a big crowd gathered at the fence and horns began honking on South Executive Avenue, Eisenhower would take refuge in one of the Secret Service guard booths. He would wait there until the crowd went away, then resume practicing.

In 1954, the U.S. Golf Association installed a putting green outside the Oval Office. It had a small sand trap on one side and two holes. Sheltered by thick bushes, it enabled Eisenhower to practice without being bothered by spectators.

But another problem surfaced. Squirrels. The squirrels who lived on the White House grounds dug holes in the putting green to bury their acorns.

When the patience of the chief executive became exhausted, staff members began live-trapping the squirrels and

Eisenhower practices putting under the watchful eye of his
grandson David.   DWIGHT D. EISENHOWER LIBRARY

releasing them far, far away. This created another problem.
Displeased nature lovers formed a "Save the White House
Squirrels Fund" and began campaigning for the preservation
of the squirrels. All squirrel operations at the White House
were halted.

Squirrels or not, Eisenhower made frequent use of the putting green. Since it was just beyond his office door, he could
duck out at just about any time during the day for a few minutes of stroking the ball. After Eisenhower left office in 1961,
a visitor to the Oval Office noted that sections of the carpeting

still displayed the puncture marks made by the cleated shoes Eisenhower had worn for his putting sessions.

The men who have been elected president have been active in a wide range of sports and recreational activities. Thanks to the many facilities offered by the White House, and the willingness of the occupants to create and install new ones, each president has been able to maintain his sporting interests during his term of office.

7

On Guard

The White House has always presented a special problem for the officials who are responsible for protecting the president and his family. The mansion must be made easy to approach and enter for the thousands who take public tours and for the throngs of official guests who visit daily. But at the same time, the White House must be so secure that no one posing a threat to the president could hope to gain entrance.

The job of protecting the Executive Mansion and the grounds is the chief mission of the Uniformed Division of the U.S. Secret Service. Established in 1922 at the request of President Warren G. Harding, the force was originally known as the White House Police. It was renamed the Uniformed Division in 1977.

Officers of the Uniformed Division are assigned to protect not only the White House complex and other presidential offices, the president and members of his immediate family, but also the vice president and members of the vice president's family, and the vice president's residence and foreign diplomatic missions.

The Uniformed Division of the U.S. Secret Service includes
female officers.   GEORGE SULLIVAN

Members of the Uniformed Division are on duty at the
sentry booths at all White House gates. These are called fixed
posts. Officers also patrol the White House grounds on foot and
in vehicles. Guard dogs sometimes accompany the officers on
patrol.

The officers maintain a security system that is considered one of the most advanced in the world. The White House itself is ringed by stone pillars and an iron-railing fence that is eight feet high. The ten vehicle entrances are closed off by solid steel, crash-proof gates. Before 1976, the gates were made of wrought iron. After a gate-crashing incident on Christmas Day, 1974, the change to steel was ordered. A man rammed his automobile into one of the Pennsylvania Avenue gates. Saying he was wired with explosives, he managed to keep the Secret Service agents at bay for four hours before he was captured. He was later sentenced to eighteen months in jail for destroying government property—the gates.

Surrounding the gates and the iron-railing fence is the White House's first line of defense—a low wall of reinforced concrete barriers, each weighing 5,000 pounds. Installed in 1983, these barriers are meant to stop any bomb-laden vehicle before it reaches the fence or gates.

The concrete barriers, iron fence, and steel gates represent only one aspect of the White House security system. Intruders can be detected by pressure sensors that dot the White House lawns, and that trigger an alarm when disturbed.

The White House complex is protected from the air, too. A cache of ground-to-air missiles is hidden nearby. Planes and helicopters from National Airport, just a few miles away, are under orders to stay away from the White House. From a command center in the Old Executive Office Building next to the White House, security officers monitor all aircraft using the airport. If a plane should veer from its established flight pattern and head for the White House, the security officers have less than a minute to decide whether to fire at the aircraft.

Nowadays, White House visitors must use either of two

Concrete barriers along Pennsylvania Avenue, weighing
5,000 pounds, defend the north end of the White House.

GEORGE SULLIVAN

Steel White House gates have replaced those of wrought
iron. GEORGE SULLIVAN

gates. One is located on East Executive Avenue, which was
closed to vehicles in 1986, and leads to the East Wing. The
other visitor gate is on Pennsylvania Avenue at the northwest
corner of the White House grounds.

Anyone using these gates must pass through a magnetome-
ter, a technical term for a metal detector, for the detection of
weapons. Specially trained dogs sniff vehicles for explosives.

Many of the people using the gates are White House employees, each of whom has been carefully screened. The name
of any prospective employee is first sent to the Federal Bureau
of Investigation for what is known as special inquiry. FBI

The White House security force includes dogs.
GEORGE SULLIVAN

agents at offices throughout the United States conduct a background investigation of the person. The agents talk with the friends, relatives, and neighbors of the prospective employee. His or her work history is reviewed, and references are checked.

The background investigation can take several months. While the FBI makes no recommendation on whether to hire a person, a background check that turns up anything unfavorable or suspicious can easily kill an individual's chance for employment.

Members of the Uniformed Division staff the White House sentry booths, or fixed posts. This is the main gate on Pennsylvania Avenue. GEORGE SULLIVAN

Once a person is hired, he or she is issued a plastic-coated identification badge. It bears a photograph of the employee and is color-coded. The color corresponds to the employee's importance and areas of the White House the person is permitted to enter.

A blue badge is the kind every employee would like to have. With a blue badge, the employee has the run of the White House and the neighboring Old Executive Office Building.

Orange and brown badges limit where one can go. Secret Service guards are stationed at various points to check badges. A wearer of a brown badge, for example, is not permitted in the blue-badge zone.

Badges have been developed with great thought and care to prevent counterfeiting. Each employee's photograph is covered with a translucent hologram, a laser-generated image recorded on photographic film. The hologram on the badge worn by media representatives has a lacelike design. When the badge is bent, the lace turns from red to yellow to green.

Officers of the Uniformed Division on duty keep a wary eye on the sidewalk outside the Northwest Gate. Protestors of every sort—feminists and farmers, nuclear-freeze supporters and war veterans, abortion advocates and abortion foes—are usually to be found there. They are drawn not only by the thought of what the White House represents but also by the cluster of television cameras on the White House lawn inside the fence.

Most people demonstrate for only a short time. They picket or hand out leaflets to passersby, most of whom are tourists, and then leave.

Those picketing have to abide by federal regulations stating that signs must be made of paper or cardboard and cannot measure more than 3 feet by 20 feet. Also, signs may not be held within three feet of the fence in front of the White House.

There is also a handful of die-hard protestors who demonstrate day in and day out for months or even years. These individuals sometimes live in tents or makeshift structures erected in Lafayette Park, which is just across Pennsylvania Avenue from the White House.

Federal law also regulates the size of the structures that can be built in the park. None can be taller than four feet. During the winter of 1986 to 1987, two men built a seven-foot igloo in the park's southwest corner. As it was nearing completion, the two were arrested for violating the park's structure regulations. The arresting officers tore down the igloo.

The igloo was illegal not only because of its size but because it was an enclosed structure that could pose a threat to the

Protestors are a daily concern for White House security forces.
GEORGE SULLIVAN

96

White House, Park Police Officer Lieutenant William Hall told the *Washington Post.* "If you have something that can conceal a large charge, or a missile launcher, that is definitely a problem."

Despite all of the security precautions, slip-ups occasionally occur. Take what happened on January 20, 1985, the day of Ronald Reagan's second inauguration. Because of the inaugural, Washington was wrapped in the tightest security in its history. Sewers along the route of the inaugural parade had been screened by security forces with bomb-sniffing dogs. Manhole covers had been sealed shut.

The president was to deliver his inaugural address from behind a clear plastic, bulletproof shield. He would be wearing what he jokingly called his long underwear—lightweight bulletproof clothing.

Robert Latta, a forty-one-year-old water-meter reader from Denver, Colorado, was barely aware of all the security precautions. Latta was a tourist, visiting Washington for the inauguration. Other tourists had told him that the Smithsonian Institution and the White House were the best places to visit.

Early Sunday morning, the day the president was to take the oath of office, Mr. Latta appeared at one of the entrance gates to the White House. He inquired about the visitors' tour. There would be no tour that day, he was told.

Then Mr. Latta noticed the red-coated Marine Band filing in through another gate. Mr. Latta, who was wearing a tan overcoat over a dark suit, fell in step behind the band members and breezed through the gate.

"Maybe I can attend the swearing-in ceremony," Mr. Latta was thinking as he followed the band up the curving driveway and into the White House. The musicians left their instruments

Robert Latta, who managed to walk through a
White House gate without being halted.

WIDE WORLD

on the ground floor and went upstairs. Mr. Latta was carrying
a bag with a book in it. He left the bag with the instruments
and followed the musicians upstairs.

The first floor of the White House, the State Floor, is used
by the first family for entertaining. Mr. Latta looked around
and peered into the various rooms. If he wasn't supposed to be
there, he thought, somebody would say something to him.

After Mr. Latta had spent about fifteen minutes milling around with members of the band, somebody did say something to him. A man in a dark suit came up to him and asked, "Do you have a ticket? Do you have an invitation?"

When Mr. Latta admitted he did not, he was taken into custody and questioned by the Secret Service. "They wanted to know everything about me," Mr. Latta said later.

Mr. Latta was placed under arrest and spent six days in jail. Psychiatrists examined him while he was there. Finally he was released and allowed to return home to Denver.

Afterward, Mr. Latta said that he didn't know it was illegal to wander into the White House—especially on one of the most important days on the presidential calendar. It was fun, he said, and he would do it again. "Only I wouldn't want to break the law," he added.

The Secret Service unit of the Treasury Department was established in 1865 to combat counterfeiting, which had become a very serious problem during the Civil War. By the war's end, between one-third and one-half of all U.S. paper currency in circulation was counterfeit. The newly formed Secret Service helped to stem the flood of bogus money.

In 1901, President William McKinley was assassinated in Buffalo, New York. McKinley was the third American president killed in thirty-six years. (Abraham Lincoln was assassinated in 1865; James Garfield, in 1881.) The public and Congress demanded that protection be provided for the president. Congress assigned the Secret Service to do the job. In 1906, legislation was passed making presidential protection a Secret Service responsibility. But it was not until 1951 that legislation making the Secret Service a permanent organization of the federal government was passed by Congress and signed by the president.

Today, the president and all members of the president's family have details of special agents assigned to them. These agents are nonuniformed.

While their primary job is protecting the president, members of the Secret Service are also assigned to protect the vice president; the immediate families of the president and vice president; the president-elect and vice president–elect and their immediate families; any former president and his wife; the widow of any former president until her death or remarriage; any children of a former president until they reach the age of sixteen; major presidential and vice presidential candidates; and visiting heads of foreign states or foreign governments.

When protecting members of the first family, Secret Service agents are more concerned about the possibility of a kidnaping than an assassination attempt. Their anxiety has increased in recent years with the growth of international terrorism and the possibility that a terrorist group might attempt to seize and hold a member of the president's family.

Agents seldom let family members out of their sight. In the White House on Christmas morning when the president and his family are opening their gifts, Secret Service agents are on duty just outside their private rooms.

In November 1968, when Richard Nixon was elected, his daughter Julie was attending Smith College in Northampton, Massachusetts. A Secret Service agent was posted outside her dormitory room and went with her any time she left the dorm. When Julie went out on a date, an agent always went along.

Amy Carter was nine years old in 1977, when Jimmy Carter

became president. When Amy went off to school each morning, a Secret Service agent accompanied her, and then spent the day with her in her fourth-grade classroom.

Members of presidential families sometimes grow tired of having Secret Service agents always a step away. They long for privacy; they want the Secret Service to leave them alone.

During Richard Nixon's term of office, the family once took a trip to California. While there, Mrs. Nixon decided to spend a few days visiting an old friend in Los Angeles. She told the Secret Service that she wanted to make the visit herself, without any agents along.

When the Secret Service protested, Mrs. Nixon relented and gave permission for an agent to follow her in a second car. The other agents, those regularly assigned to guard Mrs. Nixon, were instructed to follow far behind her, so far behind that Mrs. Nixon would never realize that they were there.

The constant presence of Secret Service agents can be awkward, too, for sons and daughters of the president who happen to be of dating age. Luci Johnson, who dated—and eventually married—Pat Nugent during her father's term, once tried to solve this problem by eluding her Secret Service coverage.

Luci and Pat were invited to attend a party in a private home in Washington. When the couple went into the party, Luci's agents remained outside. Then Luci and Pat sneaked out a back entrance without the agents knowing it. They spent the evening together on the town.

When Luci's Secret Service detail learned what had happened, they were enraged. They had nothing to say to Luci and Pat when the couple returned to the White House. Pat escorted Luci to the family quarters upstairs. When Pat came back down, the agent in charge of the Secret Service detail was there to meet him. He grabbed the young man by the front of his jacket and slammed him up against a wall. He held him there while he explained how he might have endangered the life of the president's daughter and jeopardized the jobs of several Secret Service agents. Luci and Pat never tried that trick again.

This incident is recounted in *Protecting the President,* a book by Dennis V. N. McCarthy, who retired in 1984 after a twenty-year career with the Secret Service. Says McCarthy: "One might argue that a young couple in love and about to be married deserve a night out alone every once in a while without the Secret Service. Unfortunately, however, in today's world a round-the-clock security detail is one of the prices children of presidents must pay for living in the White House."

A series of events that took place after Ronald Reagan took office in 1981 led to much tighter White House security. On March 30, 1981, Mr. Reagan was walking to his car from the banquet room of a Washington hotel when he was shot by twenty-four-year-old John W. Hinckley, Jr. A bullet entered the president's body under the left arm. He was rushed to the hospital, where doctors worked feverishly and saved his life.

Three other people were wounded in the attack. A bullet struck White House Press Secretary James Brady, and he was left partially paralyzed. A Secret Service agent and a Washington, D.C., police officer were the other victims.

As a result of the attack, Mr. Reagan took the advice of the Secret Service and began wearing a bulletproof vest in any situation where danger might lurk. The Secret Service added a vehicle filled with agents armed with machine guns to every presidential motorcade. Before the motorcade draws up to a

President Reagan waves, then looks up before being shoved into his limousine by members of his Secret Service detail after being shot outside a Washington hotel in March 1981.

presidential function, agents with metal detectors have screened all of the guests for weapons.

White House security was also affected following a tragic incident that occurred in the Mideast on October 23, 1983. A dynamite-laden pickup truck with a suicide driver at the wheel smashed through a gate and several barriers. It rammed into the Marine barracks in Beirut, Lebanon, detonating its explosive cargo. More than 240 servicemen died.

What happened in Beirut made Washington more security-conscious than it had been in years. "We've had bombings of federal buildings, but the Beirut bombing was a new type of threat," John Jester, the man in charge of security for most federal buildings in Washington told the *Washington Post.* "It makes you think, 'How are you going to stop that kind of person?'"

It was shortly after the truck-bombing in Beirut that the concrete barriers went up around the White House.

Another incident took place less than two weeks later, this time in Washington. On November 7, 1983, at about 11:00 P.M., a powerful bomb exploded in a corridor on the second floor of the U.S. Capitol outside a conference room near the Senate Chamber. The Senate had been scheduled to work late that night but adjourned unexpectedly at about 7:00 P.M. Otherwise, there would have been deaths and injuries.

Two other incidents involved gun-toters outside the White House. On December 22, 1983, White House policemen arrested a man who approached the East Gate carrying two rifles. The rifles were not loaded, but the man was carrying ammunition. He told the officers that the rifles were gifts for the president.

A more serious incident took place three months later, on

These aren't merely attractive planters outside the White House East Gate. They are designed to stop a truck as big as 9 tons traveling at 30 miles an hour. GEORGE SULLIVAN

the night of March 16, 1984. A man walking along the sidewalk outside the iron fence that separates the South Lawn from South Executive Avenue seemed suspicious to Secret Service officers. When one officer approached him, the man reached into his coat and produced a sawed-off shotgun. An agent drew his gun and fired, wounding the man.

In the past, even the recent past, presidents and their families were not nearly as security-conscious as they must be

President Lyndon Johnson walks his dogs on the White House grounds. Because of tighter security, no modern-day president can think of acting so freely.

LYNDON BAINES JOHNSON LIBRARY

today. Lyndon Johnson often led newspaper reporters on rambling walks around the White House grounds. John Kennedy was known to slip away from his Secret Service guards to visit friends in Georgetown. Dwight Eisenhower used to practice golf strokes on the White House lawns. Harry Truman frequently took brisk walks down Pennsylvania Avenue.

No president would think of acting so freely today. Countless changes have been made in the way presidents do things. For example, when foreign dignitaries arrived for state dinners in their limousines, it used to be the custom for the president to step out onto the White House's North Portico and greet them. That put him in full view of anyone who happened to be on the sidewalk along Pennsylvania Avenue outside the fence. Nowadays the president greets guests indoors or behind a special screen. More and more, battle-zone thinking is intruding upon the life of those who occupy the White House.

The emphasis on security causes some grumbling among White House visitors. They don't like seeing the president greeting state visitors behind a big screen. They don't like going through metal detectors. Many remember when a flowerpot was just a flowerpot.

Still, the White House is more open than the residences of most other chiefs of state. Visitors from foreign countries often remark how little security there is.

Index

Page numbers in *italics* refer to illustrations.

About the Author

George Sullivan is a respected and well-established author of young adult books. He has written over eighty books, covering subjects from sports to computers to Navy attack planes. He is active professionally, with memberships in PEN, the Authors Guild, and the American Society of Journalists and Authors. He taught nonfiction writing at Fordham University and has contributed to leading popular magazines, children's magazines, and the *World Book Encyclopedia*.

Mr. Sullivan lives in New York City.